WIZARD
JOKES

Smarties titles available

WIZARD JOKES

By
PETER ELDIN

Illustrations by
DAVID MOSTYN

Robinson Children's Books

First published in the UK by Robinson Children's Books,
an imprint of Constable & Robinson Ltd, 2002

Constable & Robinson Ltd
3 The Lanchesters
162 Fulham Palace Road
London
W6 9ER
www.constablerobinson.com

ISBN 1-84119-383-6

Printed and bound in the EU

10 9 8 7 6 5 4 3

INTRODUCTION

If you want to be a witch or a wizard, the best magic is knowing how to make people laugh. We have collected hundreds of the wackiest, silliest and most spell-binding jokes in the whole world. Some of them are as old as Merlin himself, others have been conjured up specially — they are so new that not even Dumbledore has heard them yet.

Do you know what a wizard wears to a tea party? Or what you call an owl with a toupee? Have you ever wondered why wizards wear pointed hats or what a baby witch is called? You can find all the side-splitting answers inside.

Plus we've raided a wizard's library to bring you lots of spoof book titles, 'What do you call a Wizard . . .' gags, wizard Doctor, Doctor and Knock Knock howlers. If you look carefully you'll even meet a schoolboy wizard called Harry Pitta!

So what are you waiting for? Enjoy reading this book and be prepared for a few surprises!

What does a wizard wear to a tea party?
A tea shirt.

Did you hear about the wizard who crossed a
rooster with a cow and got a Cock-A-Doodle-
Moo?

Old Wizard: You've heard of the great wizard
called Merlin?
Young Wizard: Oh yes.
Old Wizard: What do you think he'd be doing
now if he were still alive?
Young Wizard: Drawing his old-age pension.

What do you call an owl with a toupee?
Hedwig.

What happens to a wizard's ale when he drinks it?
He makes it disa-beer.

There's a new alarm clock especially for vain wizards.
It doesn't ring, it applauds.

Passport Officer (to wizard): Why are you standing on your head?
Wizard: Because some idiot has stuck my passport photograph in upside down.

Why did Harry potter?
Because he didn't feel like rushing!

A young lad from the village went up to the castle to be interviewed for the job as a wizard's assistant.

'You'll get fifty pounds a week to start,' said the wizard. 'Then, after six months you'll get a hundred pounds a week.'

'OK,' said the boy , 'I'll come back in six months.'

What do you get if you cross a wizard with a farmer?

Someone who can turn a herd of cows into a field.

Did you hear about the wizard who dreamed he was eating an enormous marshmallow?
When he woke up his pillow had disappeared.

Did you hear about the wizard who had a turned-up nose?
Every time he sneezed he blew his hat off.

What's the difference between a wizard and the letters K,E,S,A,M?
One makes spells, the other spells 'makes'.

Did you hear about the inquisitive wizard?
He took his nose apart to see what made it run.

How did the wizard improve the taste of salt?
He sprinkled it over some chips.

On what day does a wizard cook himself some eggs and bacon?
On fry-day.

Why did the wizard get out some sugar and milk to watch television?
Because they were showing a cereal.

What's the difference between a wizard and a biscuit?
You can't dip a wizard in your tea.

Which schoolboy wizard never goes to see a barber?
Hairy Potter.

What do you get if you cross a snake with a magician?
Abra-da-cobra.

Notice on a wizard's door: I've just disappeared for a few minutes.

What goes 'oowt tiwt'?
An owl flying backwards.

What does a wizard get if he crosses a board game with a sack and a person?
Ludo Bagman.

Why did the wizard have a blancmange in one ear and a jelly in his other ear?
He was a trifle deaf.

What do you get if you cross a schoolboy wizard with a flat bread?
Harry Pitta.

Why is a red-haired mad wizard like a biscuit?
Because he's a ginger-nut.

Why did the wizard levitate a pig?
Because he wanted the price of bacon to go up.

Farmer: How I can stop my cock from crowing on a Sunday morning?
Merlin: Eat it on Saturday.

What did the wizard get when he crossed a hyena with a gravy cube
An animal that made a laughing stock of itself.

What is grey and hairy and lives on a wizard's face?
A mousetache.

What do you get if you cross a schoolboy wizard with a golfer?
Harry Putter.

Wizard: I want an eye of newt.
Shop Assistant: Certainly, sir.
Wizard: And some dried bat's blood.
Shop Assistant: Yes, sir.
Wizard: Have you got frog's legs?
Shop Assistant: No sir, I always walk like this.

How did the wizard make a sausage roll?
He pushed it.

Why did the wizard take a fortnight to make a spell?
It was a slow-motion-potion.

What do you get if you cross a battle with a bolt?
A warlock.

Seen in a wizard's bookcase:
How to Become Invisible by C.U. Knott.

Which schoolboy wizard is yellow and greasy?
Harry Butter.

Why do wizards drink tea?
Because sorcerers like cuppas.

What does a wizard get if he crosses a pound
coin with a drainage channel?
Quidditch.

Seen in a wizard's bookcase:
Searching for the Stone by Phil O'Soffa.

What did the wizard say when he made his
jeans float in the air?
'It's a Levi-tation.'

What is the name of a man boiling in a
wizard's cooking pot?
He's called-Ron.

Why did the wizard wear a pointed hat?
Because he had a pointed head.

What does a wizard get if he crosses pigs
with skin growths?
Hogwarts.

Seen in a wizard's bookcase:
How I Do Magic by Ivor C. Crett.

What do you get if you put wings on a dog in a vehicle?
A flying car-pet.

What do you call a witch who goes to the beach but is scared of the sea?
A chicken sand-witch.

Seen in a wizard's bookcase:
Magic For Mad Magicians by X. Centrix.

What do you call a wizard with a rabbit up his trouser leg?
Warren.

What do racing witches use?
Vroomsticks.

Wizard: To keep them secret I write all my spells in invisible ink.
Assistant: What colour?

Doctor, doctor! My baby's just swallowed my magic wand, what should I do?
Just wave your hands in a mysterious manner until I get there.

What do you call a wizard with a lavatory on his head?
John.

What do you call a witch with two lavatories on her head?
Lulu.

Why did the witch shut her eyes when she looked in the mirror?
She wanted to see what she looked like when she was asleep.

Why do wizards wear large shoes?
Because of their amazing feats.

What do you call a wizard with a spade on his head?
Doug.

What do you call a wizard without a spade on his head?
Doug-less.

Wizard: Waiter, I'll have a chop; no — make it a steak.
Waiter: I'm only a waiter, sir. You're the wizard.

What do you call a wizard on his knees?
Neil.

Among the many strange things on a shelf in the wizard's den were two skulls, one large and one small.

'What's this?' asked the wizard's assistant as he picked up the larger skull.

'That', said the wizard, 'is the skull of Julius Caesar.'

'And what is the small one?'

'That is the skull of Julius Caesar when he was a child.'

A large notice was posted outside the theatre: 'The Wizard is coming!'

A week later the sign was changed to 'The Wizard will be here on Wednesday'.

On Tuesday morning the sign was 'The Wizard is here!'

Wednesday morning a new sign was put up: 'The Wizard will be on stage at 8pm tonight.'

By seven fifty-five the theatre was packed. Everyone was on the edge of their seats in anticipation.

At eight o'clock precisely the lights dimmed, there was a hush in the auditorium, the curtains opened — and there on the stage was a large sign which read: 'The Wizard has vanished!'

Seen in a wizard's bookcase:
How to Perform a Spectacular Memory Act by Ivor Gett.

King Arthur was walking through the castle grounds when he saw Merlin planting razor blades in his potato patch.
'What are you expecting to grow, Merlin?' asked the king.
'Chips!' said Merlin.

What goes abra-ha-ha-ca-ha-ha-da-ha-ha-bra-ha-ha – bonk?
A wizard laughing his head off.

What do you call a wizard in a space ship?
A flying sorcerer.

Old wizards never die; they just go away for
a spell.

Seen in a wizard's bookcase:
Tricks That Amaze by Miss Terry.

Magic Words:
Hocus Pocus,
Fish bones choke us.

Wizard: Do you know why they are not going to make magic wands any longer?
Assistant: No, why?
Wizard: Because they're long enough already.

Seen in a wizard's bookcase:
Do You Like Magic? by Frank Lee Noe.

What are baby witches called?
Halloweenies.

Why do witches fly on broomsticks?
Because vacuum cleaners are too heavy.

Wizard: I wave my magic wand and the ten ton elephant has disappeared.
Boy: It's up your sleeve.

What do you call a witch standing at the side of the road with her thumb up in the air.
A witch hiker.

Seen in a wizard's bookcase:
How to Turn Base Metals Into Gold by Al Kemmy.

What happened to the lizard in the wizard's garden pond?
He had him newt-ered.

What did the wizard get when he crossed a horse with a skunk?
Whinney the Pooh.

Seen in a wizard's bookcase:
How Is It Done? by Ida Noe.

What is the favourite form of transport for a sorceress?
Witchcraft.

What do you get if you cross a witch with an ice cube?
A cold spell.

What game did Merlin and King Arthur play?
Knights and crosses.

What do witches use pencil sharpeners for?
To keep their hats pointed.

Why did the wizard eat little bits of metal?
He wanted to have a staple diet.

Seen in a wizard's bookcase:
How Does a Wizard Perform Magic? by
Howard Eyeno.

What did the wizard say when he showed his
magic wand?
I'm a mystic, and this is m'stick.

Seen in a wizard's bookcase:
I Think I Know How It's Done by Ivan Ideer.

What did the wizard get when he crossed a mole with a hedgehog?
A tunnel that leaked.

How do wizards dress on a cold day?
Quickly!

What do you call a witch with spots?
An itchy witchy.

What's the nice thing about being a wizard?
You can have anything you wand.

Why is a magic wand black in the middle?
To keep the white ends apart.

How can you make a tall wizard short?
Borrow all his money.

If it takes ten wizards half an hour to eat a
ham, how long will it take twenty wizards to
eat half a ham?
It depends upon whether they're professional
wizards or 'am-a-chewers.

Knock knock.
Who's there?
'Allo.
'Allo who?
Alohomora — oh, don't bother, the door's just opened!

Knock knock.
Who's there?
Howard.
Howard who?
Howard you like to see my new spell?

Knock knock.
Who's there?
Madge.
Madge who?
Madge E. Quand.

Knock knock.
Who's there?
Moira.
Moira who?
Moira see your spells the moira dislike them.

Knock knock.
Who's there?
Lettuce.
Lettuce who?
Lettuce show you a spell.

Sign at a wizard convention:
We came,
We saw,
We conjured.

What do you call two witches who share a broomstick?
Broom-mates.

What happens to a witch who loses her
temper whilst flying on her broomstick?
She flies off the handle.

Seen in a wizard's bookcase:
Black Magic by Sue Pernatural.

Why will you have problems if you see
identical twin witches?
You won't be able to tell which witch is which.

What do you call a nervous sorceress?
A twitch.

How do witches lose weight?
They join Weight Witches.

Why won't a witch wear a flat cap?
Because there's no point to it.

Did you hear about the wizard who had three pairs of glasses?
One pair for indoors, one pair for outdoors, and one pair for looking for the other two.

What noise does a witch's breakfast cereal make?
Snap, cackle and pop.

Did you hear about the wizard who gave up fortune telling?
He decided there was no future in it.

What happened to the stupid wizard who put
his false teeth in the wrong way round?
He ate himself.

How do wizards tell the time?
They look at their witch watches.

Seen in a wizard's bookcase:
Producing a Lady from Nowhere by Sheila
Peer.

Why did the wizard wear a yellow robe to the
Halloween party?
He was going as a banana.

What happened to the wizard who brushed his teeth with gunpowder?
He kept shooting his mouth off.

What do you get if you cross a dinosaur with a wizard?
A Tyrannosaurus hex.

What happened when the wizard turned a naughty boy into a hare?
He's still rabbiting on about it.

Why did the wizard turn the naughty girl into a mouse?
Because she ratted on him.

What is evil and bearded and lives under the sea?
A wizard with an aqualung.

Why did the wizard wear red, white and blue braces?
To keep his trousers up.

What do you get if you cross a river with an inflatable wizard?
To the other side.

What is the first thing a wizard does in the morning?
He wakes up.

What do you call a wizard who's black and blue all over?
Bruce.

What do you call a wizard lying in the gutter?
Dwayne.

What do you call a wizard who sits on a bonfire?
Guy.

What do you call a wizard who lies on the floor?
Matt.

What do you call a wizard who has been dead and buried for thousands of years?
Pete.

Why does a wizard clean his teeth three times a day?
To prevent bat breath.

What happened to the wizard who ran away with the circus?
The police made him bring it back again.

What do you call a wizard who has fallen into the sea in a barrel?
Bob.

What kinds of wizards have their eyes
closest together?
The smallest ones.

What kinds of wizards can jump higher than a
bus?
All kinds – buses can't jump.

If a wizard were knocked out by Dracula in a
fight, what would he be?
Out for the Count.

What would happen if you threw lots of eggs
at a wizard?
He would be egg-sterminated.

What did the wizard say at the end of a long,
hard day?
I'm going gnome.

Seen in a wizard's bookcase:
When a Wizard Knocks on Your Door by
Wade Aminit.

Wizard: Doctor, doctor, I snore so loudly I keep myself awake!
Doctor: Sleep in another room then.

Wizard: Have you put the cat out?
Witch: Was he burning again?

Seen in a wizard's bookcase:
Wizard from Another Planet by A. Lee-En.

There was an old wizard from Brazil
Who always ate more than his fill
He thought it no matter
That his waistline grew fatter
But he burst. Doesn't that make you ill?

A witch as bald as a bat
Spilt hair tonic over the mat
It's grown so much higher
She can't see the fire
And she thinks that it's smothered her cat.

A witch and a wizard from Rye
Courted for years side by side.
He said, 'Dear we've tarried
Why don't we get married?'
'Cos no one would have us,' she cried.

Seen in a wizard's bookcase:
A Wizard's Biography by Eli D. Constantly.

Witch: Why do you keep losing your temper?
Wizard: Because it's all the rage!

Witch: Why have you stopped playing cards
with my sister?
Wizard: Well, would you play with someone
who cheats all the time, is a poor loser and
keeps tearing up the cards?
Witch: No I wouldn't.
Wizard: No, well nor would she.

Witch: I want you to come round the world
with me on a broomstick.
Wizard: Are you taking me for a ride?

Wizard 1: I don't think much of your toad.
Wizard 2: Never mind, eat the vegetables instead.

Did you hear about the witch who met a wizard in a revolving door?
They've been going round together ever since.

Did you hear about the wizard who turned his friend into an egg?
He kept trying to poach his ideas.

Did you hear about the very well behaved little wizard?
When he was good his father would give him a penny and a pat on the head. By the time he was sixteen he had £25 and a totally flat head.

Did you hear about the wizard who can sculpt lots of things out of skull bones? Apparently he has a high degree of witchcraftsmanship.

Wizard: Doctor, doctor, I'm having trouble with my breathing.
Doctor: I'll give you something that will soon stop that.

Doctor: Don't worry about your health – you'll live until you're eighty.
Wizard: I am eighty.
Doctor: There, what did I tell you?

Wizard: Doctor, doctor, I tend to flush a lot.
Doctor: Don't worry, that's just a chain reaction.

Wizard: Doctor, doctor, I need something to keep my falling hair in.
Doctor: How about a matchbox.

Wizard: Doctor, doctor, I keep thinking I'm an elastic band.
Doctor: Stretch yourself out on the couch.

Seen in a wizard's bookcase:
Make Money from Rich Wizards by Marie Mee.

A wizard went to the doctor one day complaining of headaches.
'It's because I live in the same room as two of my brothers,' he said. 'One of them has six goats and the other has four pigs and they all live in the room with us. The smell is terrible.'
'Well couldn't you just open the windows?' asked the doctor.
'Certainly not,' he replied. 'My bats would fly out.'

Two wizards in a car were driving along and the police were chasing them for speeding. One said 'What are we going to do?' The other replied, 'Quick, turn the car into a side street.'

The wizard who had invented a flying carpet was interviewed for a local radio station. 'What's it like, Merlin, to fly on a magic carpet?' asked the radio presenter.
'Rugged,' replied Merlin.

The wonderful Wizard of Oz
Retired from business becoz
What with up-to-date science
To most of his clients
He wasn't the wiz that he woz.

Why did the stupid witch keep her clothes in the fridge?
She liked to have something cool to slip into in the evening.

Why did the wizard keep his wand in the fridge?
He was going through a cold spell.

What has handles and flies?
A wizard in a rubbish bin.

Did you hear about the witch who invented a magic lift?
It's called a spell-e-vator.

Why do cats prefer wizards to witches?
Because the sorcerers often have milk in them!

What do you call a warlock who tries to stop fights?
A peacelock!

What did the doctor say to the witch in hospital?
'With any luck you'll be able to get up for a spell.'

What do you call a witch who climbs up walls?
Ivy.

What goes cackle, cackle, squelch, squelch?
A witch in soggy trainers.

What goes cackle, cackle, boom?
A witch in a minefield.

What did the young witch say to her mother?
'Can I have the keys to the broom tonight?'

What does a witch enjoy cooking most?
Gnomelettes.

Knock knock.
Who's there?
Witch.
Witch who?
Witch witch would you like it to be?

Why do witches have stiff joints?
They get broomatism!

What do you get if you cross a wizard and an iceberg?
A cold spell!

Why did the wizard keep turning into Mickey Mouse?
He kept having Disney spells!

Why did the young witch have such difficulty writing letters?
She had never learnt to spell properly!

Why didn't the witch sing at the concert?
Because she had a frog in her throat!

RIBET RIBET!

What do you do if a witch in a pointy hat sits
in front of you at the cinema?
Miss most of the film!

How do you get milk from a witch's cat?
Steal her saucer!

What do you get if you cross a sorceress
with a millionaire?
A very witch person!

Why do witches ride on broomsticks?
Because it's quicker than walking!

What kind of jewellery do witches wear on their wrists?
Charm bracelets!

Seen in a witch's bookcase:
Never Make a Witch Angry by Sheila Tack.

When can you tell if the witches are carrying a time bomb?
You can hear their brooms tick!

How do you make a witch float?
You take two scoops of ice cream, a glass of coke and one witch!

Why did the witch join the football club?
Because she heard they were looking for a
new sweeper!

Why are witches' fingernails never longer
than 11 inches?
Because if they were 12 inches they'd be a
foot!

What is the best way of stopping infection
from witch bites?
Don't bite any witches!

What happened to the witch with an upside down nose?
Every time she sneezed her hat blew off!

What does a witch do if her broom is stolen?
She calls the flying squad!

Why did the witches go on strike?
They wanted sweeping reforms!

What kind of tests do they give in wizard school?
Hex-aminations!

When a wizard falls into a pond, what is the first thing that he does?
Gets wet!

Why did the witch feed her cat with pennies?
She wanted to put some money in the kitty!

What does a wizard do when it rains?
Gets wet!

Which Harry can puts spells on people and is
made of leaves?
Harry Potter (The leaves were just a plant!)

Who turns the lights off at Halloween?
The light's witch!

What do you call a witch's cat that never comes when he's called?
Impussible!

Now you see it, now you don't, now you see it, now you don't – what are you watching?
A witch's cat walking over a zebra crossing!

Did you hear about the wizard who crossed a snake with a bird and got a feather boa?

What do you call a wizard with a car on his head?
Jack!

MAG IC

What do you call a witch with a cat on her head?
Kitty!

What do you call a witch with a bunch of holly on her head?
Carol!

What do you call a wizard with a paper bag on his head?
Russell!

What do you call a wizard with a seagull on his head?
Cliff!

What do you call a wizard with a crane on his head?
Derek!

What do you call a wizard with a map on his head?
Miles!

What do you call a wizard with a car number plate on his head?
Reg!

What do you call a wizard with a wig on his head?
Aaron!

What do you call a witch with a radiator on her head?
Anita!

What do you call a wizard with a mat on his head?
Neil!

What do you call a witch with slates on her head?
Ruth!

What do you call a witch with a spring on her head?
April!

What do you call a wizard with some cat scratches on his head?
Claude!

What do you call a wizard with a stamp on his head?
Frank!

What do you call a witch with a breeze on her head?
Gail!

What do you call a witch with a tennis racket on her head?
Annette!

What do you call a wizard with a kilt on his head?
Scott!

What do you call a witch with a tortoise on her head?
Shelley!

What do you call a witch with a twig on her head?
Hazel!

What do you call a wizard with a legal document on his head?
Will!

What do you call a wizard with a double-decker bus on his head?
The deceased!

What do you call a wizard who forgets to put his underpants on?
Nicholas!

What do you call a wizard with a tree growing out of his head?
Ed-Wood!

What do you call a witch with a sheep on her head?
Baa-Baa-Ra!

What did the stupid wizard call his pet zebra?
Spot!

What do you call a wizard who wears tissue paper trousers?
Russell!

Why did the witch with a ponytail go to see her doctor?
She was a little hoarse!

What do you call a witch flying through the skies?
Broom Hilda!

What do you call a wizard made from toilet paper?
Louie!

What do you call a witch with sandpaper on her head?
Sandie!

What do you call her sister who lives at the seaside?
Sandie Shaw!

What do you call a wizard who steals cows?
A beef burglar!

Why did the wizard hold his boot to his ear?
Because he liked sole music!

What did the wizard say when he accidentally
burped while playing football?
'Sorry, it was a freak hic!'

Wizard: Waiter, this soup tastes funny!
Waiter: Then why aren't you laughing?

Wizard: Waiter, what's this fly doing in my
soup?
Waiter: It looks like it's learning to swim.

Wizard: Waiter, there's a caterpillar on my salad.
Waiter: Don't worry sir, there is no extra charge.

Wizard: Waiter, there is a fly in my soup.
Waiter: Don't worry sir, that spider on your bread will soon get him!

Wizard: Waiter, there is a small slug in this lettuce.
Waiter: I'm sorry sir, would you like me to get you a bigger one?

Wizard: Waiter, bring me something to eat and make it snappy.
Waiter: How about a crocodile sandwich sir?

Wizard: Waiter, this coffee is terrible, it tastes like earth!
Waiter: Yes sir, it was ground yesterday!

Wizard: Waiter, is there soup on the menu?
Waiter: No, sir, I just wiped it off!

Wizard: Waiter, this egg is bad.
Waiter: Don't blame me sir, I only laid the table!

Wizard: Waiter, there is a slug in my salad!
Waiter: I'm sorry sir, I didn't realise you were a vegetarian!

Wizard: Waiter, there is a cockroach on my steak!
Waiter: They don't seem to care what they eat do they sir!

Witch: Waiter, there is a slug in my salad!
Waiter: Sorry madam, no pets allowed!

Witch: Waiter, there is a wasp in my pudding!
Waiter: So that's where they go in winter!

Witch: Waiter, there is a fly in my wine!
Waiter: Well you did ask for something with a little body in it!

Wizard: Waiter, there is a fly in my soup!
Waiter: Yes sir, that's the manager: the last customer was a wizard as well!

Witch: Waiter, there's a fly in my soup!
Waiter: Yes, it's the rotting meat that attracts them!

Witch: Waiter, do you serve snails?
Waiter: Sit down, madam, we serve anyone!

Wizard: Waiter, what's this spider doing in my alphabet soup?
Waiter: Learning spells!

Witch: Waiter, what is this creepy-crawly doing in my salad?
Waiter: Not him again, he's in here every night!

What is a wizard's favourite bird?
An ostwitch.

What do you call a wizard who is green and slimy and lives under rocks?
A lizard.

An angry witch burst into the baker's shop and said:

'I sent my black cat in for two pounds of biscuits this morning but when I weighed them there was only one pound. I suggest you check your scales.'

The baker looked at her calmly for a moment and then replied:

'Madam, I suggest you weigh your cat.'

What do you call a wizard with dandruff?
A blizzard.

How do you greet a three-headed dog?
Hello, hello, hello!

Did you hear about the stupid wizard who always drove his car in reverse?
It was because he knew the town backwards.

Wizard 1: Do you have holes in your underpants?
Wizard 2: No, of course not!
Wizard 1: Then how do you get your feet through?

What's the most important thing to remember when boiling up a spell?
Never lick the spoon.

Have you heard of the wizard who is so short sighted he can't get to sleep unless he counts elephants?

How did the wizard stop a cold from going to his chest?
He tied a knot in his neck.

What do you get if you cross an owl with a skunk?
A bird that stinks to high heaven.

How can you tell if a witch has been sleeping in your bed?
There are holes in the head board.

Why was the wizard annoyed when he bumped into an old friend?
They were both driving their cars at the time.

Why did the witch call both her children Ed?
Because she figured that two Eds were better than one.

How do you keep a stupid wizard happy for hours?
Give him a piece of paper with PTO written on both sides.

How do you make a stupid wizard burn his ear?
Ring him up while he is ironing!

Did you hear about the wizard who tried to iron his curtains?
He fell out of the window.

Why did the witch have her hair in a bun?
Because she had her nose in a hamburger.

A witch woke her husband in the middle of the night. 'There's a burglar downstairs eating the cake that I made this morning.'
'Who shall I call,' her husband replied, 'police or ambulance?'

On which side does an owl have the most feathers?
On the outside.

Why did the witch fix her bed to the chandelier?
Because she was a light sleeper.

Why can't the deaf wizard be sent to prison?
Because you can't condemn someone without a hearing.

Did you hear about the stupid wizard who had a bath put in?
The plumber said, 'Would you like a plug for it?'
The wizard replied, 'Oh, I didn't know it was electric.'

Policeman: What gear were you in at the time of the accident?
Witch: Oh, the usual: black cloak, pointy hat.

What's the difference between a lazy wizard and a kilo of lard?
One's a fat lot of good and the other is a good lot of fat.

Why did the wizard decide to become an electrician?
To get a bit of light relief.

Did you hear about the wizard who was so lazy, he went around with his mouth open to save himself the trouble of yawning?

Did you hear about the vain wizard who was going bald?
The doctor couldn't do a hair transplant for him, so he shrunk his head to fit his hair.

What has two heads, three hands, two noses and five wands?
A wizard with spare parts.

Why do old wizards cover their mouths with their hands when they sneeze?
To catch their false teeth.

How can you tell an old wizard from a young wizard?
An old wizard can sing and brush his teeth at the same time.

The wizard's wife gave birth to twin baby girls, but it was difficult to tell which witch was which.

Two wizards were having an argument.
'I didn't come here to be insulted' yelled one.
'Really? Where do you normally go?'

How can a wizard double his money?
By folding it in half.

How do wizards dress in winter?
Quickly!

What's the difference between a witch with
a toothache and a rainstorm?
One roars with pain, the other pours with
rain.

Did you hear about the wizard who crossed a
sheep and a rainstorm and got a wet blanket?

Did you hear about the wizard who crossed a sheep dog and a bunch of daisies and got Collie-flowers?

Did you hear about the wizard who crossed a centipede with a parrot and got a walkie-talkie?

Did you hear about the wizard who crossed a kangaroo with a mink and got a fur jumper with pockets?

Did you hear about the wizard who crossed a zebra with a donkey and got a zeedonk?

Did you hear about the wizard who crossed a cow and a camel and got lumpy milkshakes?

What's green, has four legs and two wands?
Two seasick wizards.

Why did the wizard put bread in his shoes?
Because he had pigeon toes.

A wizard in a swimming pool was on the very top diving board. He lifted his arms and was about to dive when the lifeguard came running up, shouting,
'Don't dive! There's no water in that pool!'
'It's OK,' replied the wizard, 'I can't swim!'

Why did the witch wear a green felt pointy hat?
So she could walk across snooker tables without being seen!

What did the pig say when the man grabbed him by the tail?
'That's the end of me.'

What's the difference between a witch's cat and a witch's frog?
The cat has nine lives, but the frog croaks every night!

What's a witch's favourite pop group?
Broomski Beat!

What has six legs and flies?
A witch giving her cat a ride!

Why do wizards paint the bottoms of their feet yellow?
So they can hide upside down in a bowl of custard.

How do you get a wizard into the fridge?
1. Open door.
2. Insert wizard.
3. Close door.

To whom do wizards always take off their hats?
Hairdressers!

What steps would a wizard take if a madman came rushing at him with a knife?
Great big ones!

How do you get a witch into the fridge?
1. Open door.
2. Remove wizard.
3. Insert witch.
4. Close door.

Why did the wizard cross the road?
It was the chicken's day off.

Why did the wizard study magic in the aeroplane?
He wanted a higher education!

What's the difference between an American wizard an English wizard?
About 3000 miles!

Why did the wizard die with his boots on?
Because he didn't want to stub his toe when he kicked the bucket!

Did you hear about the wizard who invented a gas that could burn through anything?
Now he's trying to invent something to hold it in!

Why did the lazy wizard want a job in a bakery?
So he could loaf around!

Why did the witch feel ill when travelling?
She got broom sick!

Why did the wizard drag a cabbage on a lead?
He thought it was a collie.

Why did the wizard with only one hand cross
the road?
To get to the second-hand shop!

What do you get if you cross a dog and a
frog?
A croaker spaniel!

Wizard: Doctor, doctor. My wife thinks she's a clock!
Doctor: Well stop winding her up then!

How does a wizard make an apple puff?
He chases it round the garden.

Why did the stupid wizard give up tap dancing?
He kept falling into the sink.

Did you hear about the wizard who tried to cross the channel?
He couldn't find a long enough plank.

What happened when the witch slept under
her car?
She woke up very oily next morning.

Wizard: How much is that owl?
Shopkeeper: Ten pounds.
Wizard: OK, could you please send me the
bill?
Shopkeeper: I'm sorry, but you'll have to take
the whole bird.

What goes hoo-hoo whoosh, hoo-hoo whoosh?
An owl caught in a revolving door.

What has feathers and is bright purple?
An owl holding its breath.

What happened to the witch's cat who
swallowed a ball of wool?
She had mittens.

How many witches does it take to change a
light bulb?
Only one, but she changes it into a toad!

Why did the witch's cat want to be a nurse?
She wanted to be a first-aid kit.

What does a witch ask for when she arrives at a hotel?
Broom service.

What kind of umbrella does a wizard carry when it's raining?
A wet one.

What happened to the wizard who couldn't tell putty from toothpaste?
His windows fell out.

Where do wizards go dancing in California?
San Frandisco.

Why do owls watch the news?
To get the feather forecast.

How can you divide six potatoes among 20
wizards?
Boil them and mash them!

Did you hear about the wizard who bought a
wooden car with wooden wheels and a wooden
engine?
It wooden go!

Why did the wizard hit the clock?
Because the clock struck first.

Psychiatrist: What's on your mind?
Wizard: I think I'm a dog.
Psychiatrist: How long has this been going on?
Wizard: Ever since I was a puppy.

Why did the greedy witch go outside with her purse open?
She expected some change in the weather.

Why did the wizard go out with a prune?
Because he couldn't find a date!

What's the last thing a wizard takes off before going to sleep?
His feet off the floor!

What kind of flower grows on a wizard's face?
Tulips!

Why did the wizard run around his bed?
To catch up on his sleep!

What does an agnostic, dyslexic insomniac wizard do at night?
He lies awake and wonders if there really is a dog!

Why did the wizard throw his trousers out of the window?
He heard the newspaper boy yell 'Free Press'.

Why did the wizard tiptoe past the medicine cabinet?
He didn't want to wake the sleeping pills!

Six witches were standing under an umbrella: which one got wet?
None of them, it wasn't raining!

Why did the wizard put a clock under his desk?
Because he wanted to work overtime!

What is a witch's cat's favourite colour?
Purrrrrrrrrple!

Did you hear about the wizard who crossed
poison ivy and a four leaf clover?
He got a rash of good luck!

Did you hear about the wizard who crossed a
cheetah and a hamburger?
He got fast food!

Did you hear about the wizard who crossed a
Mustang and an elephant?
He got a convertible with a big trunk!

Did you hear about the wizard who crossed a
hula dancer with a boxer?
He got a Hawaiian Punch!

Did you hear about the wizard who crossed a clown with a goat and got a Silly Billy?

Did you hear about the wizard who crossed a vampire with a mosquito?
He ended up with a very itchy neck!

Did you hear about the wizard who crossed a chicken and a cow?
He got roost beef!

Did you hear about the witch who crossed a galaxy with a toad?
She got Star Warts!

Did you hear about the wizard who crossed a strawberry with a road and got a traffic jam?

Did you hear about the wizard who crossed a lizard and a baby?
He ended up with a creepy crawler!

Did you hear about the wizard who crossed an elephant and a rhinoceros and got an Elephino?

Did you hear about the wizard who crossed a bat and a bell?
He got a dingbat!

Did you hear about the wizard who crossed a blue cat and a red parrot and got a purple carrot?

Did you hear about the wizard who crossed a cow and a duck?
He got milk & quackers!

Did you hear about the wizard who crossed a kangaroo and a sheep and got a woolly jumper?

Did you hear about the wizard who crossed an elephant with a skin doctor and got a Pacadermatologist!

Did you hear about the wizard who crossed an octopus with a cow?
He ended up with a farm animal that could milk itself!

Did you hear about the wizard who crossed a bank with a skunk and got dollars and scents?

Did you hear about the wizard who crossed a parrot and a centipede and got a walkie-talkie?

Did you hear about the wizard who crossed a Karate expert with a pig and got pork chops?

How did the stupid wizard try to kill a fish?
He tried to drown it!

Why did the wizard bring toilet paper to the birthday party?
Because he was a party pooper!

What did the stupid wizard say when he put money in the parking meter?
Hey! Where is my gumball?

How did the stupid wizard fall on the floor?
He tripped over the cordless phone!

Why did the stupid wizard drive his truck off the bridge?
He wanted to check his airbrakes!

Why was the stupid wizard hitting his head against the wall?
Because it felt so good when he stopped!

How do you drown a stupid wizard?
Put scratch-n-sniff stickers at the bottom of the pool!

Why did the stupid wizard climb the glass wall?
To see what was on the other side!

Why did the stupid wizard open the
refrigerator door?
He wanted to see the salad dressing!

How many stupid wizards does it take to
screw in a light bulb?
Three. One to hold the bulb, and two to turn
the chair!

Why did it take the stupid wizard an hour to
eat breakfast?
Because the orange juice carton said
Concentrate!

What do you do if a stupid wizard throws a grenade at you?
Pull the pin and throw it back!

How do you confuse a stupid wizard?
Put him in a round room and tell him to sit in the corner!

How can you tell when a stupid wizard has been using the computer?
There is correction fluid all over the screen!

How did the stupid wizard break his arm while raking leaves?
He fell out of the tree!

Why did the boy wake up in the morning to find a witch on a broomstick in his bedroom? Because he left the landing light on.

A wizard was looking under the bonnet of his broken-down car.
Another driver stopped to help. 'Can I give you a hand?' he asked.
The wizard replied, 'I'd rather have a tow.'

Did you hear about the old witch who had so many wrinkles that she had to screw her hat on?

A witch came across a little boy pulling her cat's tail. 'Hey, you!' she called. 'Don't pull my cat's tail!'
'I'm not pulling!' replied the boy. 'I'm only holding on – the cat's doing the pulling!'

Why did the owl say 'moo'?
It was learning a new language!

What happens if a wizard eats yeast and shoe polish?
Every morning he'll rise and shine!

How does a wizard catch a squirrel?
He climbs a tree and acts like a nut!

How many stones can you fit in an empty
witch's hat?
One! After that it's not empty!

What are two things a wizard cannot have for
breakfast?
Lunch and dinner.

Why did the witch sprinkle sugar on her
pillow before she went to sleep?
So she could have sweet dreams.

A wizard was speeding down the road, feeling secure in a group of cars that were all travelling at the same speed. However, as they passed a speed trap, he got caught and was pulled over. The officer handed him a speeding ticket and was about to walk away when the wizard asked, 'Officer, I know I was speeding, but I don't think it's fair – there were plenty of other cars around me going just as fast, so why did I get the ticket?'

Ever go fishing?' the policeman asked the wizard.

'Ummm, yeah . . .' the wizard replied.

The officer grinned and said, 'Ever catch all the fish?'

An exhausted looking wizard dragged himself in to the Doctor's office. 'Doctor, there are dogs all over my neighbourhood. They bark all day and all night, and I can't get a wink of sleep.'

'I have good news for you,' the doctor answered, rummaging through a drawer full of sample medications. 'Here are some new sleeping pills that work like a dream. A few of these and your trouble will be over.'

'Great,' the wizard answered, 'I'll try anything. Let's give it a shot.'

A few weeks later the wizard returned, looking worse than ever. 'Doc, your plan is no good. I'm more tired than before!'

'I don't understand how that could be', said the doctor, shaking his head. 'Those are the strongest pills on the market!'

'That may be true,' answered the wizard wearily, 'but I'm still up all night chasing those dogs and when I finally catch one it's hard getting him to swallow the pill!'

A wizard walks into a restaurant and notices a large sign on the wall, '£500 IF WE FAIL TO FILL YOUR ORDER!'

When his waitress arrives, he orders elephant tail on rye. She calmly writes down his order and walks into the kitchen where the wizard hears yelling, screaming, and all sorts of commotion.

The restaurant owner comes storming out of the kitchen. He runs up to the wizard's table, slaps five £100 notes down on it and says, 'You got me that time buddy, but I want you to know that's the first time in ten years we've been out of rye bread!'

A witch goes to see the doctor. She's got a pea in one nostril, a grape in the other, and a string bean stuck in her ear. She says to the doctor, 'I feel awful.'
The doctor replies, 'It's obvious that you're not eating right!'

How far can a wizard run into a forest?
Halfway: after that he's running out!

Once there were two witch's cats racing
across the lake.
One was French, one was English. The French
one was named 'Un deux trois,' the other was
named 'One two three.'
Which cat won the race?
'One two three' because 'Un deux trois' cat
sank.

There were two owls sitting in a tree and the
first owl said, 'Man it's really hot tonight' and
the second owl replied, 'O MY GOD, IT'S A
TALKING OWL!'

What does a wizard say to improve his sight?
'Hocus focus!'

Why do wizards who scuba dive always go into the water backwards?
Because if they go in the other way, they fall in the boat!

There was a witch sitting on the steps in front of her house. Her cat was sitting beside her. A wizard came up to her. 'Hello, what's your cat's name?' he asked. 'Ben Hur.' the witch answered. 'Where'd you come up with that?' asked the wizard. 'Well, we used to call it Ben, until it had kittens.' she replied.

Phoning a wizard, the doctor says, 'I have some bad news and some worse news. The bad news is that you only have twenty-four hours to live.'

'That's bad news,' the wizard replies. 'What could be worse?'

The doctor answers, 'I've been trying to reach you since yesterday.'

What do you call a wizard who makes bowls? Harry Potter.

Did you hear about the wizard who crossed lassie with a bulldog and got a dog that bites himself and then runs for help?

Knock knock.
Who's there?
Wizard.
Wizard who?
Wizard do this more often!

Knock knock.
Who's there?
Wand.
Wand who?
Wand to come in!

Knock knock.
Who's there?
Sadie.
Sadie who?
Sadie magic words!

Knock knock.
Who's there?
Wyden.
Wyden who?
Wyden you tell me you were a wizard?

Knock knock.
Who's there?
Jane.
Jane who?
Jane-bar of Secrets.

Knock knock.
Who's there?
Too wit!
Too wit who?
Is there an owl in here?

Knock knock.
Who's there?
Harry.
Harry who?
Harry up and open the door!

Knock knock.
Who's there?
Baby owl.
Baby owl who?
Baby owl see you later, maybe I won't.

Knock knock.
Who's there?
Dozen owl go.
Dozen owl go who?
Yes it does.

What did the mayonnaise say to the wizard
who opened the refrigerator door?
'Shut the door I'm dressing!'

Wizard 1: Eat your spinach, it will put colour
into your cheeks.
Wizard 2: Who wants green cheeks?

One day a wizard was driving down the
motorway when his wife called him on his
mobile. She said, 'Be careful, I heard there
was somebody driving on the motorway the
wrong way.' And he said, ' It's not one person
– it's all of them.'

One day a little girl came home from wizard school and said to her mother, 'Today in school I was punished for something that I didn't do!' The mother exclaimed, 'But that's terrible! I'm going to have a talk with your teacher about this! What was it that you didn't do?' The little girl replied, 'My homework!'

An owl goes to a shop and asks for some birdseed. The shop assistant says, 'No, we're a bookshop.' The owl returns the next day and asks for some birdseed. The shop assistant says, 'No, we're a bookshop.' The owl comes in the next day and asks for some birdseed. The assistant says 'NO!! We're a bookshop. Next time you come and ask for birdseed I will nail your feet to the floor!' The owl leaves the shop. He comes in the next day and asks for nails. The assistant replies, 'No, we don't sell nails.'
'Got any birdseed then?'

Why do wizards feel stronger on Saturdays and Sundays?
Because all the other days are weak days.

Did you hear about the wizard who crossed a dozen eggs with a werewolf and got a giant hairy omelette?

A wizard was driving along a road when a rabbit jumped out in front of his car. He slammed on his brakes, but still he hit the rabbit and killed it. He was so upset that he began to cry. Soon, a witch stopped her car and realised what had happened.

'Don't worry,' said the witch. 'This will make everything better,' and took a spray can out of her handbag. She sprayed the dead rabbit all over until suddenly it leaped up and hopped away. Then it stopped and waved, then hopped off again. Finally it shook its paw at them one more time and then disappeared into some bushes.

'That's amazing' said the wizard. 'What is in that can?'
The witch turned the can around so that he could read the label. It said: 'HARE SPRAY: RESTORES LIFE TO DEAD HARE. ADDS PERMANENT WAVE.'

Why did the wizard eat a light bulb?
Because he was in need of light refreshment.

What's the difference between a boxer and a wizard with a cold?
One knows his blows and the other blows his nose!

Did you hear about the wizard who is so rich he has two swimming pools, one of them which is empty? It's for people who can't swim!

Did you hear about the stupid wizard who listened to a match?
He burned his ear!

Did you hear about the absent-minded wizard who went round and round in a revolving door for three hours?
He didn't know whether he was coming or going!

Wizard: Can you tell me one substance that conducts electricity?
Pupil: Why, er . . .
Wizard: Correct!

A wizard walked into a council rent office with a £5 note stuck in one ear and a £10 note in the other. He was £15 in arrears.

Did you hear about the wizard who went on a banana diet?
He didn't lose any weight, but he can't half climb trees well!

Wizard 1: It's raining cats and dogs out there.
Wizard 2: I know. I've just stepped in a poodle!

A wizard went into a shoe shop. 'I'd like some crocodile shoes, please,' he said.
'Certainly, sir. How big is your crocodile?'

Did you hear about the wizard who sat under a cow?
He got a pat on the head.

A wizard walked into a chemist shop and asked for a spray that fills a room with the smell of rotten eggs, stale socks and sour milk. 'What do you want that for?' asked the chemist. 'I've got to leave my flat this morning, and the landlord says I've got to leave it exactly how I found it!'

Did you hear about the witch whose fingernails were so long that when she picked her nose she scratched her brain?

Why did the wizard wear an extra pair of trousers when he played golf?
In case he got a hole in one.

A wizard went into a pet shop to buy an owl. He was shown an especially good one which he liked the look of, but he was puzzled by the two strings which were tied to its feet.

'What are they for?' he asked the pet shop manager.

'Ah well, sir,' came the reply, 'that's a very unusual feature of this particular owl. You see, he's a trained owl, sir. He used to be in a circus. If you pull the string on his left foot he says "Hello" and if you pull the string on his right foot he says "Goodbye".'

'And what happens if I pull both the strings at the same time?' asked the wizard.

'I fall off my perch, you idiot' hissed the owl.

Did you hear about the wizard who plugged his electric blanket into the toaster by mistake?
He spent the night popping in and out of bed.

Why do stupid wizards eat biscuits?
Because they're crackers.

Policeman: Why are you driving with a bucket of water on the passenger seat?
Wizard: So I can dip my headlights.

What has two legs, a pointed hat and flies?
A dead witch.

Wizard: I want a haircut please.
Barber: Certainly, sir. Which one?

A wizard in a restaurant was handed the
menu by the waiter who, the wizard was
worried to observe, stood by the table
scratching his bottom.
'I say, waiter,' said the wizard in disgust.
'Have you got an itchy bottom?'
'No, sir,' replied the waiter. 'Only what is on
the menu!'

If twenty wizards chase one wizard, what time is it?
Twenty after one.

A wizard walked into a pet shop.
'I'd like to buy a dog, please.'
'Certainly, sir. Any particular breed? A Red Setter, perhaps?'
'No, not a Red Setter.'
'A Golden Labrador?'
'No, not a Golden Labrador. I don't want a coloured dog, just a black-and-white one.'
'Why a black-and-white one, sir?'
'Isn't the licence cheaper?'

The witch answered a knock on the door and
found a total stranger standing on the
doorstep.

'Excuse me for disturbing you, madam,' he
said politely, 'but I pass your house every day
and I've noticed that every day you appear to
be hitting your son on the head with a loaf of
bread.'

'That's right.'

'Every day except today, when you hit him
with a chocolate gateau?'

'Well, today is his birthday . . .'

Why was the Egyptian witch confused?
Because her daddy was a mummy.

A wizard sat on a train chewing gum and staring vacantly into space, when suddenly an old woman sitting opposite said 'It's no good you talking to me: I'm stone deaf.'

Doctor: This is a most unusual complaint. Have you had it before?
Wizard: Yes, doctor.
Doctor: Well, you've got it again.

Did you hear about the wizard who went fly-fishing and caught a three-pound bluebottle?

Did you hear about the wizard who went to night school to learn to read in the dark?

Wizard: Doctor, doctor! I think I'm a dog!
Doctor: Sit down, please.
Wizard: But I'm not allowed on the furniture!

Why is a complaining wizard easy to satisfy?
Because nothing satisfies him.

Wizard: Doctor, doctor, I've only got 59 seconds to live.
Doctor: Just sit over there for a minute.

What do a tone-deaf witch and a wizard opening a tin of sardines have in common?
They both have trouble with the key.

Do old wizards always snore?
No. Only when they're asleep.

Which hand should you use to stir a boiling potion?
Neither – you should use a spoon.

Why did the wizard wear a rubber ring at night?
Because he liked sleeping on a water bed but he couldn't swim!

What should a wizard take if he is run down?
The number plate of the vehicle that hit him!

What is brown, hairy, wears round glasses
and can do magic?
A coconut disguised as Harry Potter.

Did you hear about the smelly wizard who
spent a fortune on deodorants before he
found out that nobody liked him anyway?

Wizard 1: My owl died of flu.
Wizard 2: I didn't know owls got flu.
Wizard 1: Mine flew into a car.

Two wizards went into a very dark, spooky cave. 'I can't see a thing,' said one.
'Hold my hand,' said the other.
'All right.' The first wizard reached out.
'Take off that horrible bristly glove first, though.'
'But I'm not wearing a glove . . .'

Man: Can you give me something for my baldness?
Wizard: How about this skunk potion?
Man: Will it make my hair grow back?
Wizard: No, but if you spray it all over your body, nobody will come near enough to notice that you're bald!

Did you hear about the tiny wizard who was so small his chin had a rash from his boot laces?

Do you serve wizards in this bar?
No sir, you have to bring your own.

Why are fried onions like a forgetful wizard?
They keep repeating themselves.

What's the difference between an interfering wizard and someone who's just got out of the bath?
One is rude and nosey, the other is nude and rosy.

Witch 1: My dustbin must be full of toadstools.
Witch 2: Why's that?
Witch 1: There's not mushroom inside.

What has eight legs and can't hold a tune?
Four tone-deaf wizards carol singing.

What happened when the wizard's owl swallowed a roll of film?
Nothing serious developed.

What has a black pointy hat and two wheels?
A witch doing a wheely on a skateboard.

Why did the stupid witch throw her guitar away?
Because it had a hole in the middle.

Wizard 1: Finally my years of hard work have paid off. I have just invented something that everyone in the world will want! You know how you get a nasty ring around the bathtub every time you use it, and you have to clean the ring off?
Wizard 2: Yes, I hate that.
Wizard 1: Well you need never have a bathtub ring again. I've invented the square tub . . .

Did you know that a well-brought-up witch never crumbles her bread or rolls in her soup?

Wizard: I'd like to buy an owl please. How much do they cost?
Pet shop owner: £10 apiece.
Wizard: How much does a whole one cost then?

Wizard 1: Why do you keep scratching yourself?
Wizard 2: Because no one else knows where I itch.

What did the fat wizard win when he lost 50 pounds in weight?
The No-Belly prize.

Why was the old wizard arrested for looking at sets of dentures in a dentist's window?
Because it was against the law to pick your teeth in public.

What does a wizard do if he splits his sides laughing?
Starts running until he gets a stitch.

Did you hear about the wizard who got worried when his nose grew to eleven inches long?
He thought it might turn into a foot.

Wizard: What are you reading?
Witch: It's a book about electricity.
Wizard: Oh, current events?
Witch: No, light reading.

Did you hear about the witch who was so keen on road safety that she always wore white at night?
Last winter she was knocked down by a snow plough.

Wizard 1: Why are you standing on your head?
Wizard 2: I'm just trying to turn things over in my mind.

Wizard 1: This is an amazing castle. Have you lived here all your life?
Wizard 2: Not yet.

Wizard 1: I've got a wonder watch. It was very cheap.
Wizard 2: What's a wonder watch?
Wizard 1: Every time I look at it, I wonder if it's still working.

Why did the witch take a load of hay to bed?
To feed her nightmare.

What do you call a wizard with cow droppings
all over his shoes?
An incowpoop.

How do you keep a stupid wizard happy all his
life?
Tell him a joke when he's a baby.

A wizard walked into a bar holding a dog poo
in his hand. 'Look everyone,' he cried. 'See
what I almost stood on!'

'Ugh! You smell terrible,' said the doctor to the wizard.

'That's odd,' said the wizard. 'That's what the other doctor said.'

'If you were told that by another doctor, why have you come to me?'

'Because I wanted a second opinion.'

Witch 1: What's that on your shoulder?
Witch 2: That's Tiny.
Witch 1: Looks like a reptile to me.
Witch 2: Yeah. He's my newt!

Wizard: Can you give me a room and a bath?
Hotel Manager: I can give you a room, but you'll have to bath yourself!

Witch 1: I'm very worried about your nail-biting habit.
Witch 2: Lots of people bite their nails.
Witch 1: But not six-inch rusty ones!

Wizard 1: Every time I drink a cup of tea I get a sharp pain in my nose.
Wizard 2: Try taking the spoon out of the cup.

A very large wizard got on a crowded bus. 'Is no one going to give me a seat?' boomed the wizard. A little girl stood up and said, 'I'll make a small contribution.'

Witch 1: I've just been bitten by a black cat. Should I put cream on it?
Doctor: No, it'll be miles away by now.

Did you hear about the wizard with grease stains all over his cloak?
He had a chip on his shoulder.

Wizard: Doctor, doctor, I've just swallowed a watch.
Doctor: Eat lots of prunes. That should help you to pass the time.

There were two mosquitoes watching two wizards giving blood. 'It's not fair,' said one to the other. 'They're happy to lie down and let someone drain a pint of blood, but if we zoomed down for a quick nip, they'd do their best to kill us!'

'What's the secret of living to 140?' the young wizard asked the old wizard.
'Slugs!' replied the old wizard.
'Slugs?'
'Yes! I've never eaten one in my entire life!'

'I'm sorry,' said the surgeon, 'but I left a
sponge in you when I operated last week.'
'Oh,' said the wizard, 'I was wondering why I
was so thirsty all the time.'

The young wizard wanted to know the secret
of life so he asked a wise old wizard.
'Pay me a thousand pounds and I will answer
one question!' said the wise old wizard.
The young wizard reluctantly paid him the
money: 'That's very expensive, isn't it?'
'Yes, it is,' replied the wise old wizard. 'Next
question?'

Harry Potter: How many drops of magic pong potion does it take to stink out Hogwarts?
Hermione: Quite a phew.

Witch 1: There were two chocolate cakes in the larder yesterday and now there's only one. Why?
Witch 2: I didn't switch the light on, so I didn't notice the other one.

A wizard walks into a cheese shop. 'I'd like a two-handed cheese, please.'
'What's that?' asked the shop assistant.
'The kind you eat with one hand and hold your nose with the other!'

There was a wizard named Wright,
Who instructed his son to write right;
He said, 'Son, write Wright right.
Don't write Wright as "rite":
Try to write Wright, all right?'

Wizard 1: Are you coming to my party?
Wizard 2: No, I ain't going.
Wizard 1: Didn't they teach you anything in wizard school? It's not ain't. It's I am not going, he is not going, she is not going, they are not going.
Wizard 2: Blimey, ain't nobody going?

There was a witch from Quebec.
Who wrapped both her legs round her neck!
But then she forgot
How to undo the knot,
And now she's an absolute wreck!

A girl went into a newsagents and saw a wizard hanging by one arm from the centre of the ceiling.

'What's that wizard doing there?' she asked the shop keeper.

'Oh, ignore him,' said the shop keeper. 'He thinks he's a light bulb.'

'Well, why don't you tell him he isn't?' asked the girl.

'What?' replied the shop keeper, 'and work in the dark?'

A seven-foot wizard with round shoulders, very long arms and one leg ten inches shorter than the other walked into a clothes shop.
'I'd like to see a suit that will fit me,' he told the shop assistant.
'So would I, sir,' the shop assistant replied. 'So would I.'

Wizard 1: Why are you going around telling everyone I'm an idiot?
Wizard 2: I'm sorry. I didn't know it was meant to be a secret!

Wizard: Half a kilo of kiddies, please.
Butcher: You mean half a kilo of kidneys.
Wizard: That's what I said, diddie I?

A witch was having her hair cut and noticed
that the hairdresser's hands were filthy.
When she pointed this out the hairdresser
replied, 'Yes, madam, no one has been in for a
shampoo yet.'

As a wizard was walking under a ladder, a brick fell from a hod and hit him on the head. He shouted to the builder, 'You clumsy idiot! One of those bricks hit me!'
'You're lucky,' came the reply. 'Look at all the ones that didn't!'

Wizard 1: Can I borrow your book – How to Make a Million Pounds Appear out of Thin Air?
Wizard 2: Sure. Here you are.
Wizard 1: But half the pages are missing.
Wizard 2: What's the matter? Isn't half a million enough for you?

What happened when the stupid wizard had a brain transplant?
The brain rejected him.

Wizard: Doctor, doctor, I keep seeing double.
Doctor: Take a seat, please.
Wizard: Which one?

Why do wizards paint their toenails pink?
So they can hide in cherry trees.

Witch 1: Why are you taking that steel wool home?
Witch 2: I'm going to knit myself an aeroplane.

A stupid wizard who was down on his luck, saw a sign outside a police station which read: MAN WANTED FOR ROBBERY. So he went in and applied for the job!

Have you ever seen a wizard in a cherry tree? Shows how effective their disguise is.

Why did the witch dye her hair yellow?
To see if blondes really do have more fun.

Witch 1: I like your toad. He always has a smile on his face.
Witch 2: That's because he's a hoptimist.

Why did the wizard use a tool kit instead of a wand?
Because he had a screw loose.

Wizard: Waiter, waiter, I'd like a pork chop, and make it lean.
Waiter: Certainly, sir, which way?

Why did the wizard have a piano in the bathroom?
Because he was practising Handel's Water Music.

Waiter, waiter, do you serve wizards?
No sir, they won't fit in the microwave.

What did the wizard say after spending
thousands in an expensive hotel?
'I'm sorry to leave, now that I've almost
bought the place!'

A tight-fisted wizard walks into a hotel.
'How much for a room?'
'Thirty pounds a night and extra if you have a
room with a view.'
'What if I promise not to look out of the
window?'

Hotel Owner: I hope you had a pleasant stay, sir.
Wizard: Not really. Your hotel promised bed and board, but I couldn't tell which was the bed and which was the board.

Wizard: Please call me a taxi.
Porter: OK, but you look more like a wizard to me.

What has a pointed hat and a broomstick and is found at the North Pole?
A witch with no sense of direction.

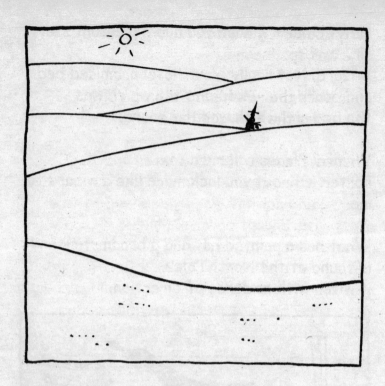

What do you call a wizard in the Sahara?
Lost.

Did you hear about the stupid witch who
tried to swim the English Channel?
She had one mile to go, but got tired and
decided to swim back.

Policeman: Did you know you were speeding,
madam?
Witch: I'm so sorry, officer. I was trying to
get home before my broomstick ran out of
fuel.

Why couldn't the witch do any magic?
She was spellbound!

How does the witch's cat stop a VCR?
It pushes the PAWS button!

There were once three wizards and they
visited a magic slide, where whatever you said
while going down it, you landed in. So the
first wizard went down and yelled 'GOLD', and
he landed in gold. Then the second wizard
went down and yelled 'SILVER', and he landed
in silver. The third wizard was having such a
good time, as he was going down he yelled
'WHEEEEEEEEEEEEE!'

Why did the wizard push his bed into the
fireplace?
He wanted to sleep like a log.

What happened to the owl who stuck his beak
in a light socket?
He got an electric bill.

What did the surgeon say to the wizard who
wanted to perform his own operation?
'All right, suture self.'

Seen in a witch's bookcase:
Going on a Witch Hunt by Count Miout.

How can a wizard's pockets be empty and still have something in them?
When they are full of holes.

Dumbledore: It cost a fortune to have Hogwarts painted.
Harry: Wouldn't it have been cheaper to have it photographed?

A wizard went into a pet shop.
'I want an owl for my little boy,' he said.
'Sorry, sir. We don't do swaps.'

Barber: How would you like your hair cut, sir?
Wizard: In complete silence.

Did you hear about the eccentric wizard who had parsnips growing out of his ears?
He was really upset – he'd planted carrots!

Wizard: Excuse me, can I try on this cloak in the window?
Shop Assistant: Why don't you use the changing room like everyone else?

Did you hear about the wizard who stole some rhubarb?
He was put into custardy.

Witch: Whisper something sweet in my ear.
Wizard: Double chocolate chip ice cream.

Where does a wizard leave his dog when he goes shopping?
In the barking lot.

What do you call a wizard with an elephant on his head?
Squashed.

There was an old witch from Dover
Who decided to knit a pullover.
But would you believe
She knitted four sleeves?
And now it only fits Rover.

What happened to the wizard who turned
into an insect?
He beetled off.

What's the difference between a rabbit who
goes jogging and an eccentric wizard?
One is a fit bunny, the other is a bit funny.

What wizards have the shortest legs?
The smallest ones.

What do you call the witch who set fire to
her gas bill?
Bernadette.

There was an old wizard called Jake
Who had a poisonous snake
It bit his head
And now he's dead
So that was the end of Jake.

Did you hear about the wizard who believed in reincarnation?
In his will he left his money to himself.

What was proved when the fat wizard was run over by a steamroller?
That he had a lot of guts.

Did you hear about the wizard who tried to cross the Loch Ness Monster with a goat?
He had to get a new goat.

Did you hear about the wizard who thought he was Dracula?
He was a pain in the neck.

Did you hear about the little wizard who thought he was Dracula?
He was a pain in the bum.

A wizard came home one day to find a ghostly figure with lots of wild hair, a long, ragged jacket and big staring eyes. 'Who are you?' asked the wizard.

'I am the ghost of Beethoven,' said the apparition.

'I don't believe you,' said the wizard. 'If you are Beethoven, perform his last movement.'

'All right,' said the ghost and fell off the piano stool.

A wizard in a cinema notices what looks like a bear sitting next to him.

'Are you a bear?'

'Yes.'

'What are you doing at the movies?'

'Well, I liked the book.'

A wizard was staying in a haunted castle and in the middle of the night he met a ghost. The ghost said, 'I have been walking these corridors for 300 years.' The wizard said, 'In that case, can you tell me the way to the toilet?'

A wizard tried to poison his wife. As she lay writhing on the floor saying 'What have you done? What have you done? What have you put in my tea?' he said, 'Oh shut up! There you go, belly-aching again!'

What did the really ugly wizard do for a living?
He posed for Halloween masks.

Why is a wizard wearing sunglasses like a rotten teacher?
Because he keeps his pupils in the dark.

Look at that bald wizard over there. It's the first time I've seen a parting with ears.

A wizard who was very upset walked in to see his doctor. 'Doctor, you've got to help me!' he wailed.

'What seems to be the trouble?' asked the doctor.

'I keep having the same dream, night after night. There's this door with a sign on it, and I push and push the door but I can't get it open.'

'What does the sign say?' asked the doctor.

'Pull,' said the wizard.

A wise old wizard was walking along whistling while balancing a television set on one shoulder and an ironing board on the other. 'How do you manage to do that?' asked a passer-by. 'It's easy,' replied the wizard. 'Just put your lips together and blow.'

A wizard went into the local department store where he saw a sign on the escalator — DOGS MUST BE CARRIED ON THIS ESCALATOR. The wizard then spent the next two hours looking for a dog.

A wizard sat playing chess with his owl in a pub. A stranger came in and sat down and in amazement watched them playing. When they had finished the game he came over. 'I'm a movie producer,' he explained as he introduced himself. 'Your owl could make a fortune in Hollywood.' The wizard just shrugged. 'He's not that clever,' he boasted. 'I've just beaten him three times in the last four games.'

My uncle must be the meanest wizard in the world. He recently found a crutch — then he broke his leg so he could use it.

Did you hear about the wizard who had B.O. on one side only?
He bought Right Guard, but couldn't find any Left Guard.

Why did the monster take a dead wizard for a drive in his car?
Because he was a car-case.

A doctor had been attending a rich old wizard for some time, but the old chap had not long to live. So the doctor advised his wealthy patient to put his affairs in order. 'Oh yes, I've done that,' said the old warlock. 'I've only got to make a will. And do you know what I'm going to do with all my money? I'm going to leave it to the doctor who saves my life.'

A wizard rushed into the doctor's surgery, jumped on the doctor's back, and started screaming 'One! Two! Three! Four! Five!' 'Wait a minute!' yelled the doctor, struggling to free himself. 'What do you think you're doing?' 'Well, doctor,' said the eccentric wizard, 'they did say I could count on you!'

A wizard who bought an owl took it back, complaining that it made a mess all over the house. 'I thought you said it was house-trained,' he moaned. 'So it is,' said the previous owner. 'It won't go anywhere else.'

A wizard standing at a bus stop was eating fish and chips. Next to him stood a lady with her little dog, which became very excited at the smell of the wizard's supper and began whining and jumping up at him. 'Do you mind if I throw him a bit?' said the wizard to the lady. 'Not at all,' she replied. So the wizard picked the dog up and threw it over a wall.

One very hot day an extremely small wizard went into a cafe, put his newspaper on a table and went to the counter. But on returning with a cup of tea he saw that his place had been taken by a huge, bearded, ferocious-looking 300-pound wizard who was over seven feet tall.

'Excuse me,' said the little wizard to the big wizard, 'but you're sitting in my seat.' 'Oh yeah?' snarled the big wizard. 'Prove it!' 'Certainly. You're sitting on my ice cream.'

A witch wanted to marry a ghost. I can't think what possessed her.

A witch telephoned her local newspaper to let them know that her cat had just given birth to 28 kittens. The reporter didn't quite hear the message and said, 'Could you repeat that?'
'I doubt it,' replied the witch.

A wizard is in a prison cell with no windows and no doors; there are no holes in the ceiling or trapdoors in the floor, yet in the morning the wardens find him gone. How did he get out? Was it magic? No, he escaped through the doorway — there were no doors remember?

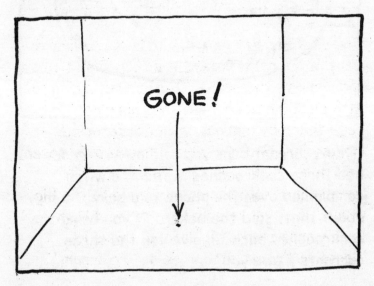

GONE!

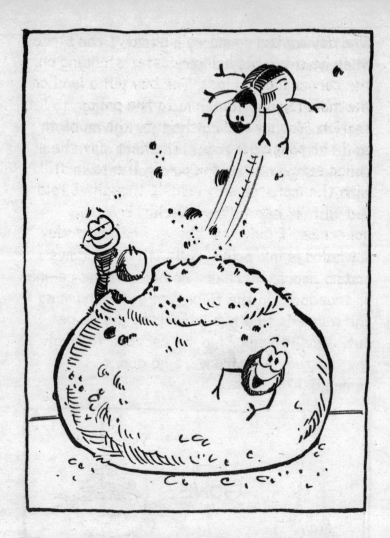

'Those currant buns you sold me yesterday
had three cockroaches in them,' a witch
complained over the phone to a baker. 'Sorry
about that,' said the baker. 'If you bring the
cockroaches back I'll give you the three
currants I owe you.'

One day a wizard was walking down the street when he saw a big hairy monster standing on the corner looking lost. The boy put a lead on the monster and took him to the police station. 'You should take him to the museum' said the police sergeant. The next day the police sergeant saw the boy in the town still with the monster on a lead. 'I thought I told you to take him to the museum' said the policeman. 'I did,' said the wizard 'and today I'm taking him to the cinema.'

What happened when a wizard crossed a
parrot with a vampire?
It bit his neck, sucked his blood and said,
'Who's a pretty boy then?'

What do you call a witch with a frog on her
head?
Lily.

What does a witch stand on after taking a
shower?
A bat mat.